THIS BOOK BELONGS TO

....

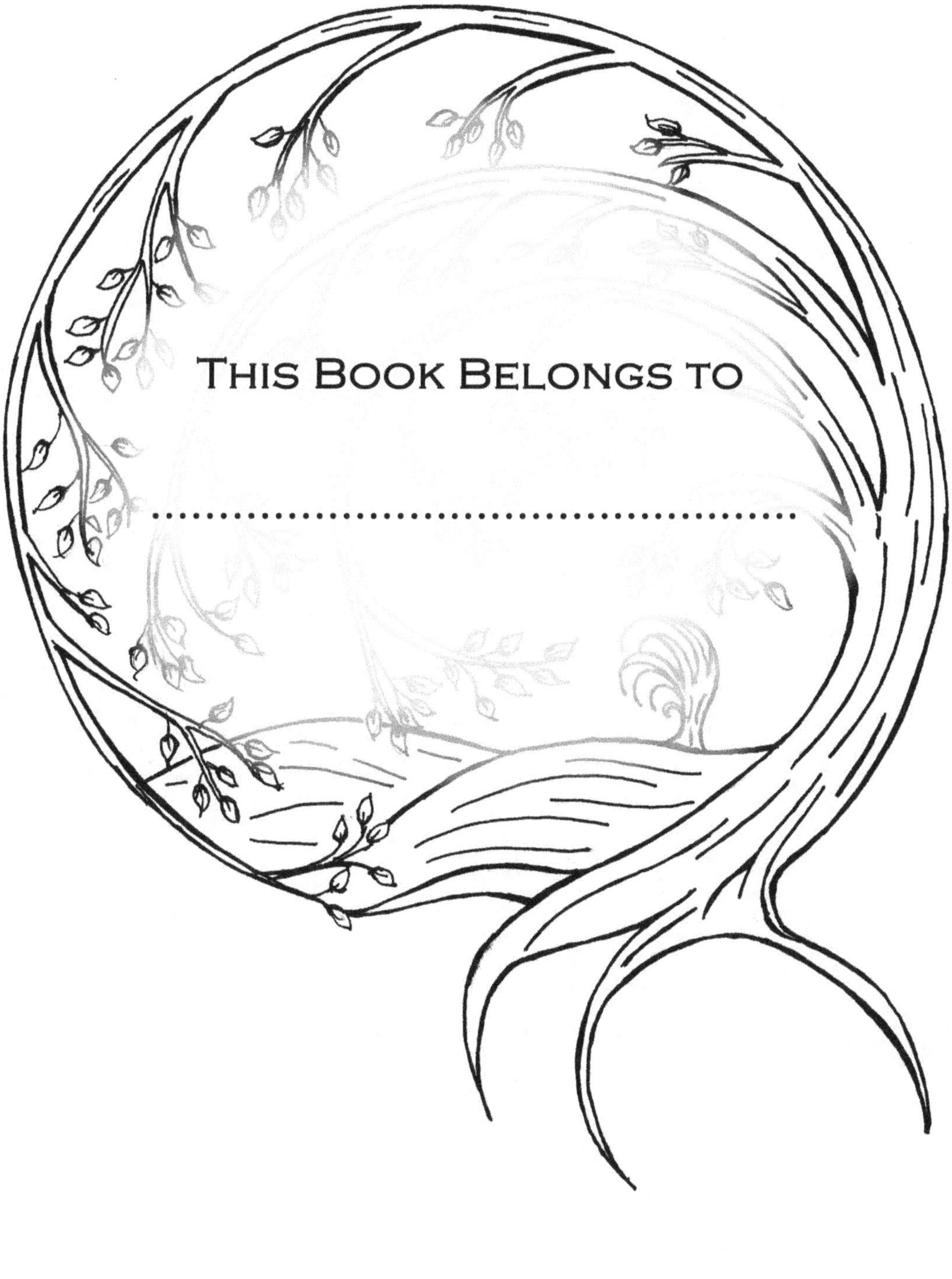

The Mystic Tree

A COLORING BOOK OF TREES

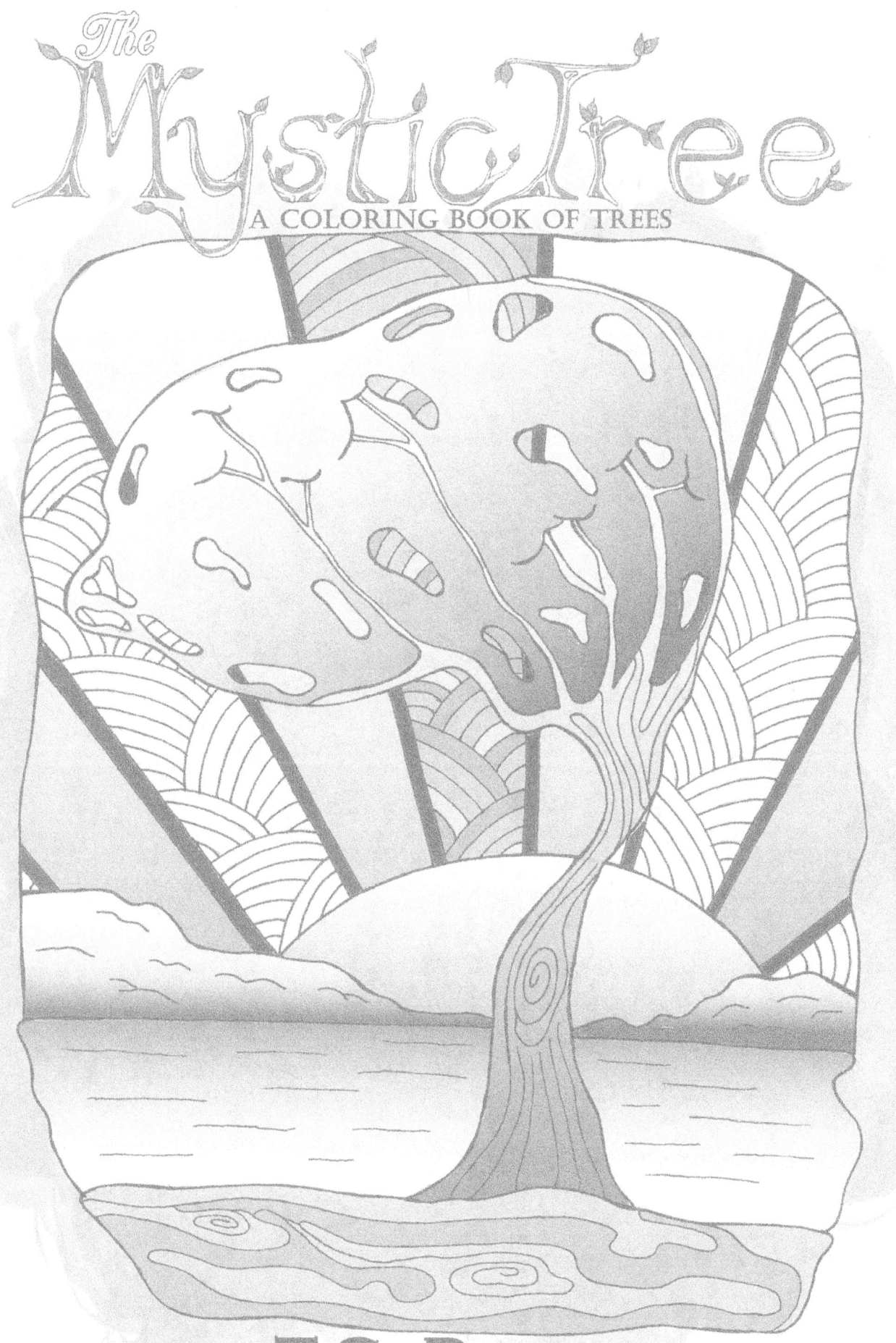

T.S. DOBSON

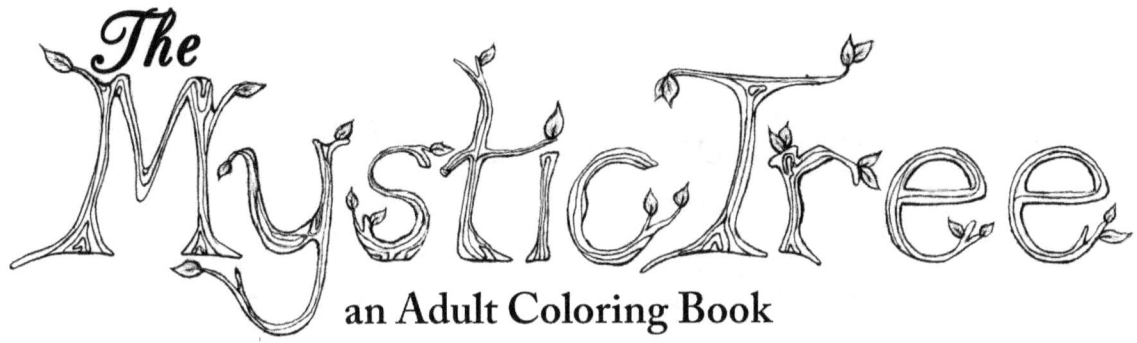

an Adult Coloring Book

ISBN-13: 978-1530436095
ISBN-10: 1530436095

Cover and Interior Art by Teresa Scott Dobson

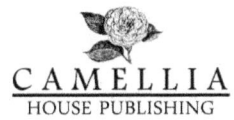

CAMELLIA
HOUSE PUBLISHING

Camellia House Publishing, Century, FL
Printed in the United States of America.

camelliahousepublishing@aol.com

Before You Get Started!

1. Put away all of the worldly distractions around you -- TV, phone, computer, etc.

2. Take out some color pencils, markers or crayons.

3. Pick a page and go with it. There's no particular order to follow.

4. When you finish a design, personalize it by signing your name anywhere on the page.

5. Find the drawing pad in the back of the book and doodle your own designs then color them!

6. Stop when you need a break, then pick it up again later.

7. When finished, if you desire, share your creations with others!

"I think the kind of landscape that you grew up in, it lives with you. I don't think it's true of people who've grown up in cities so much; you may love a building, but I don't think that you can love it in the way that you love a tree or a river or the colour of the earth; it's a different kind of love."

Arundhati Roy

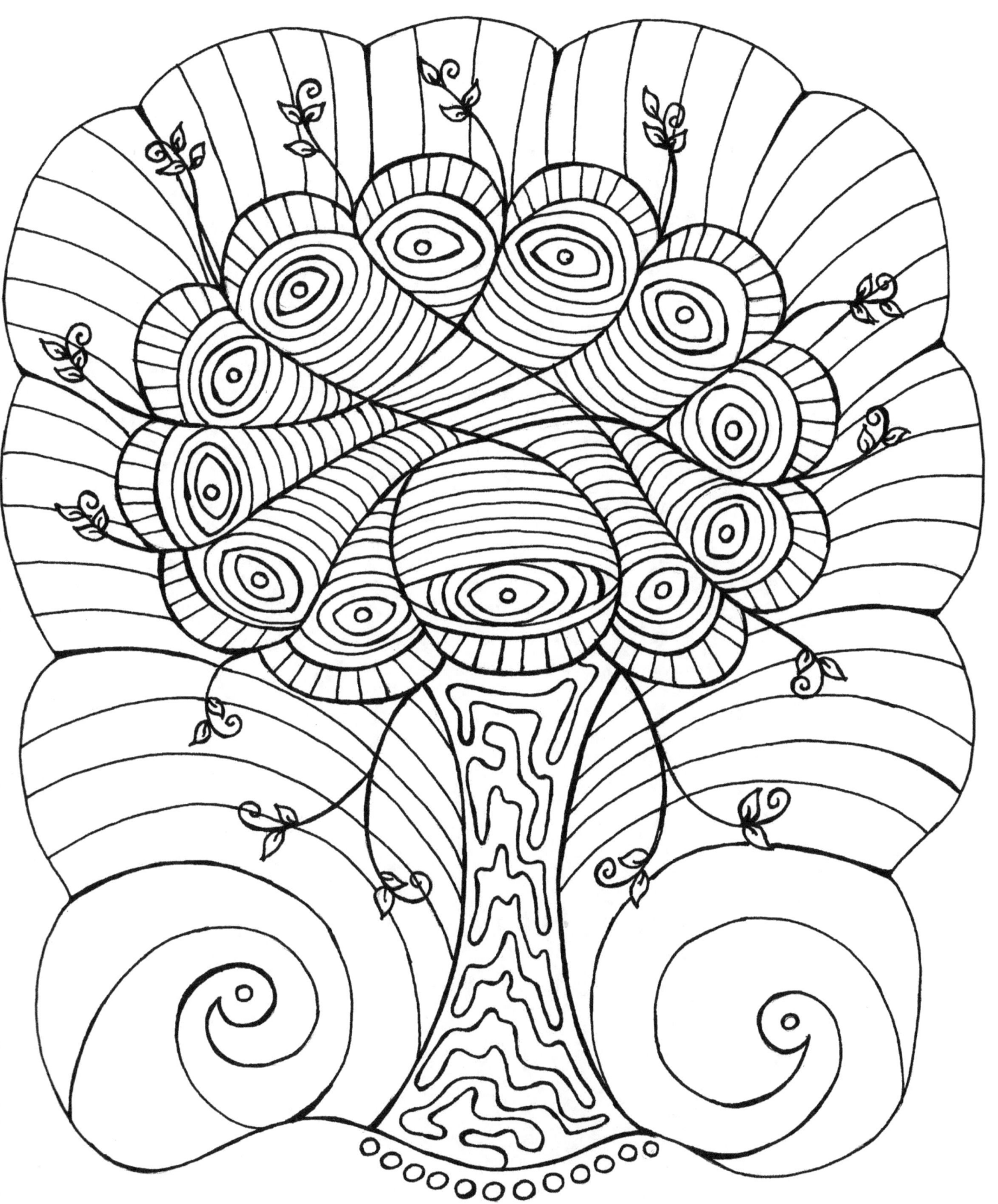

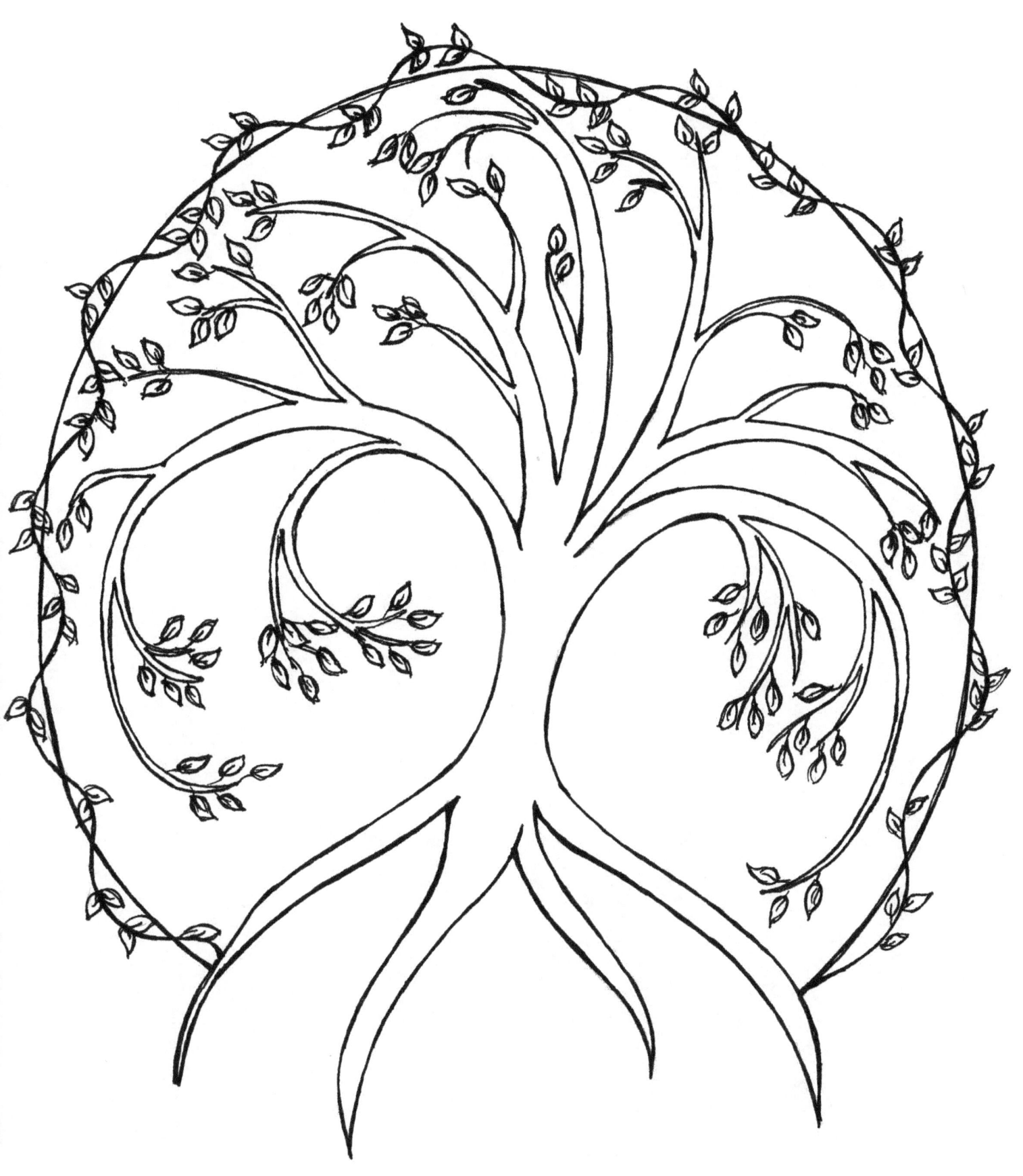

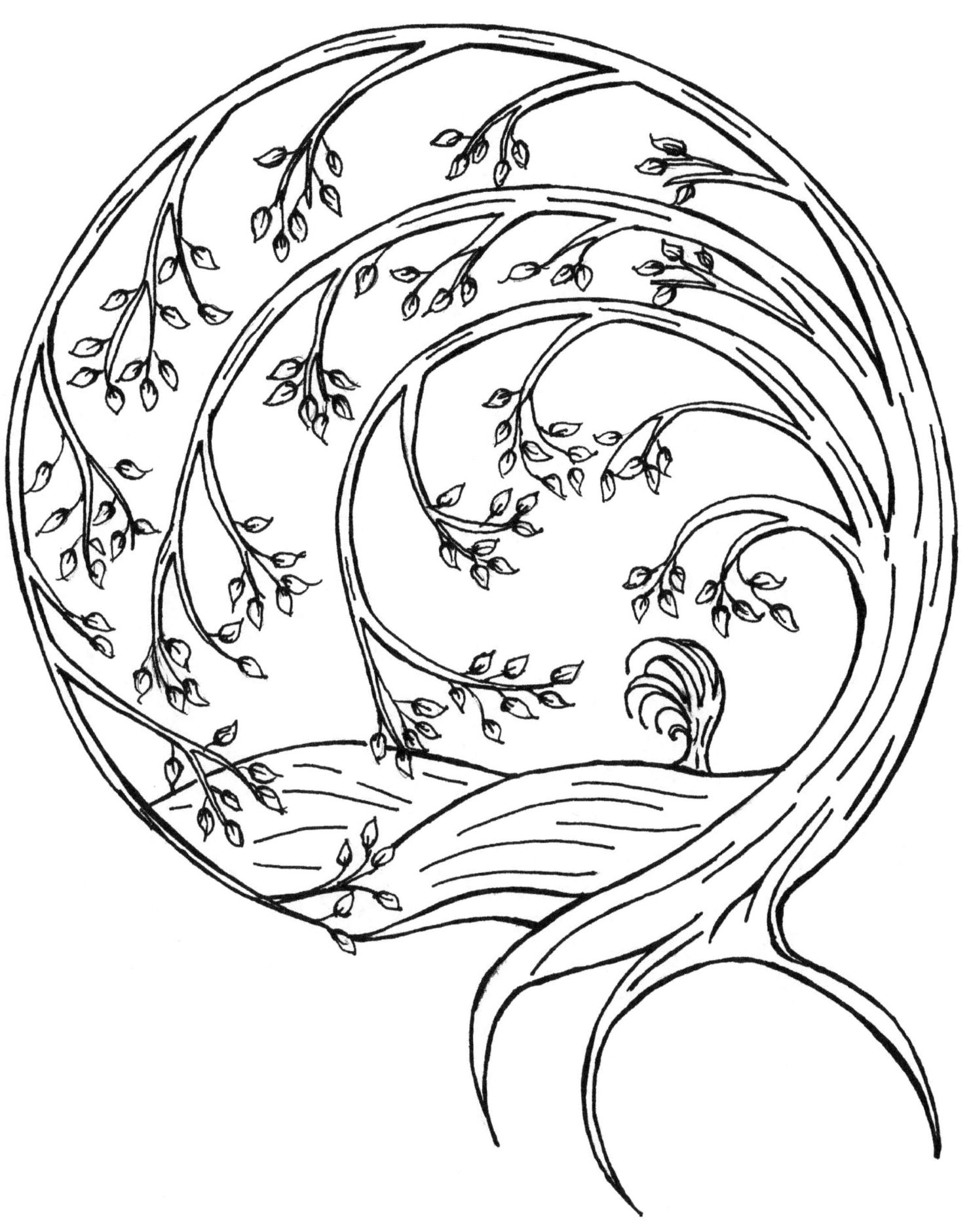

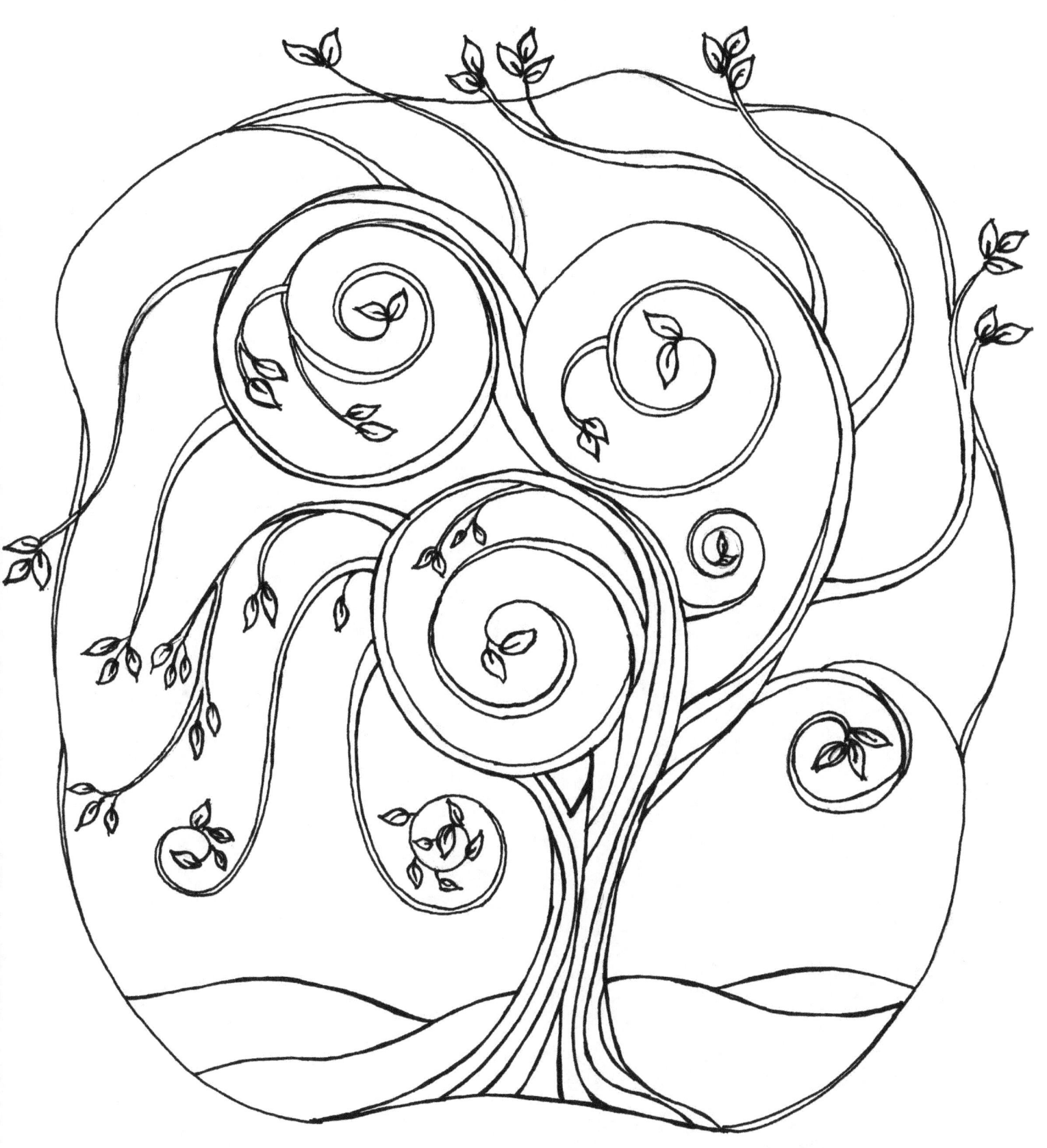

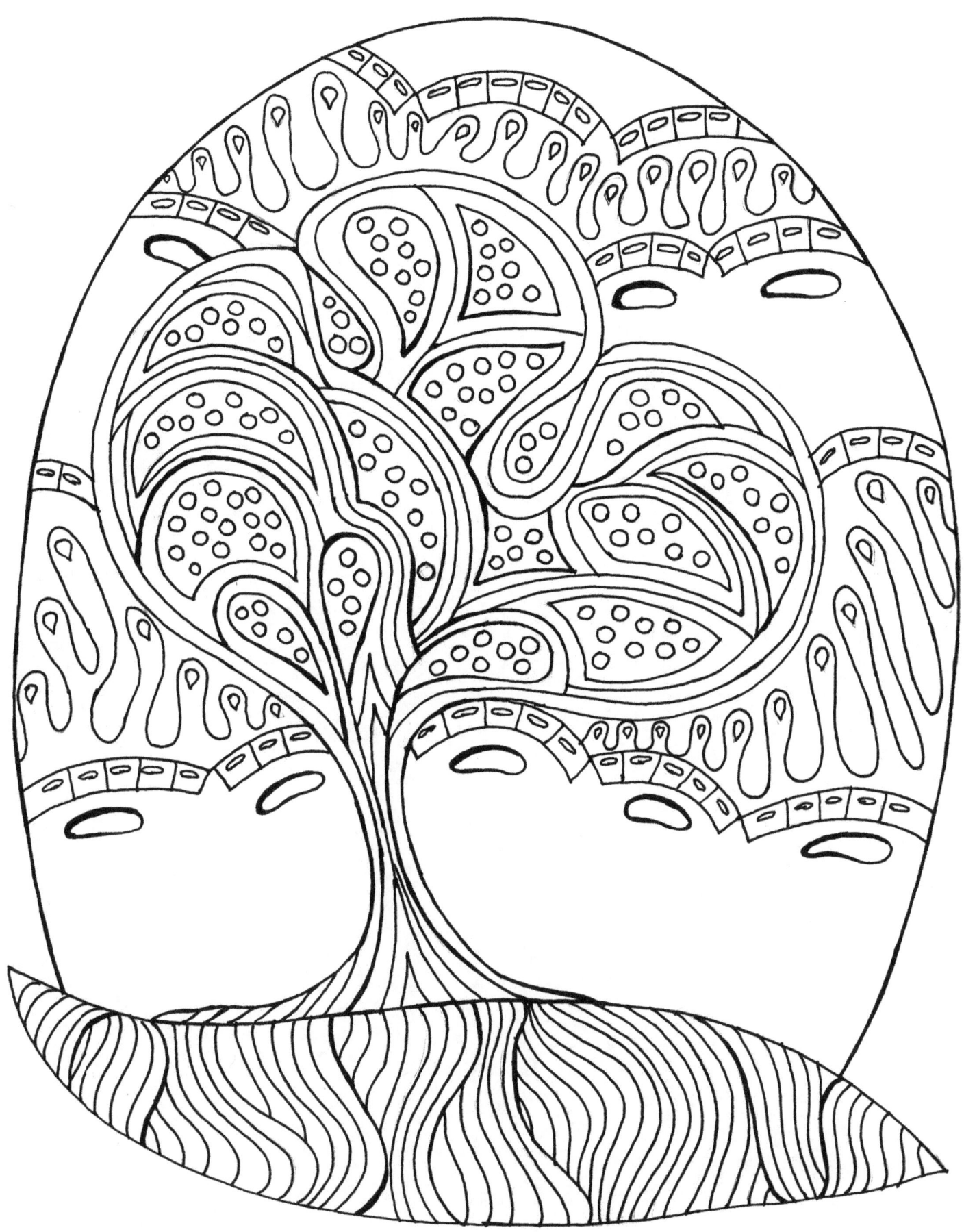

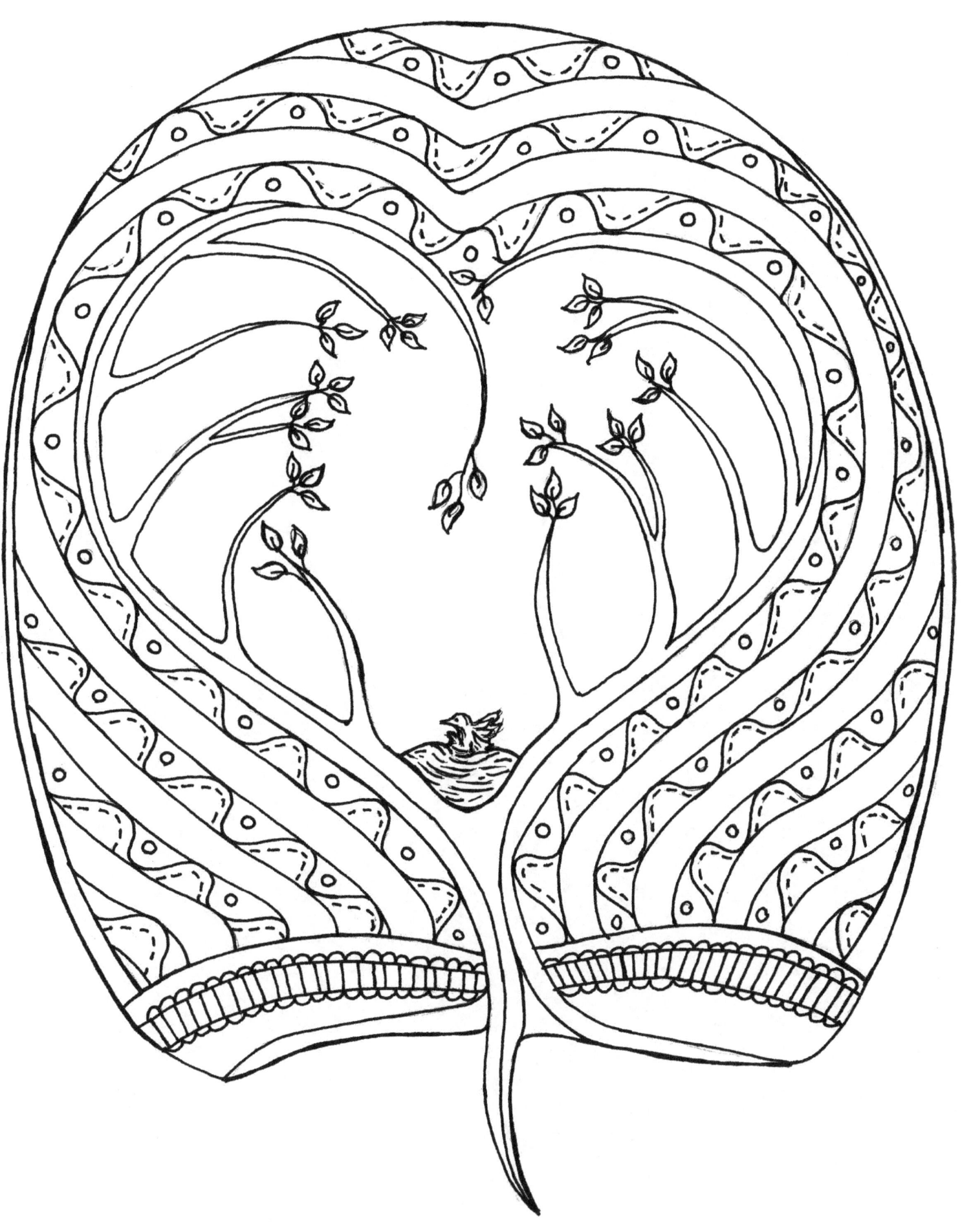

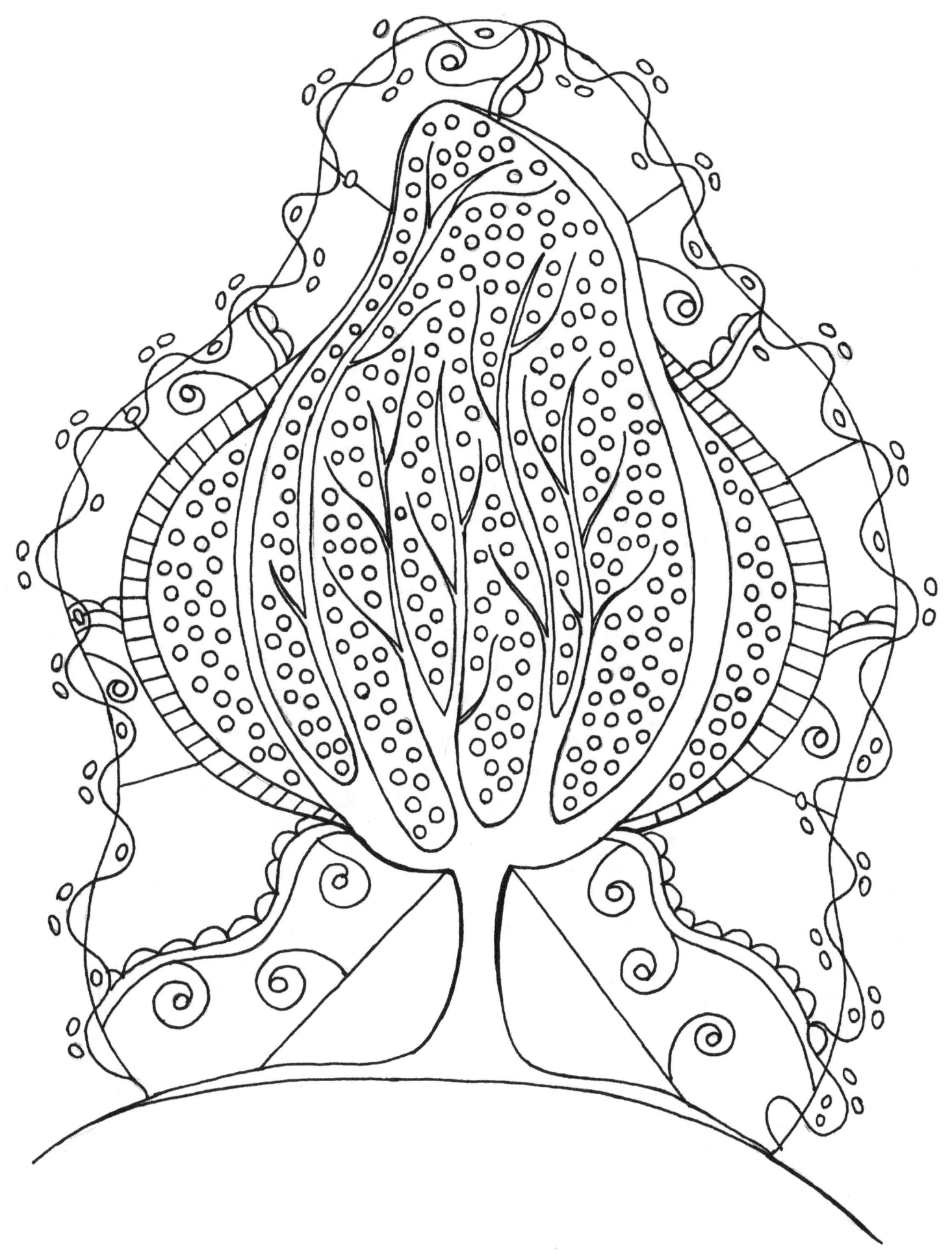

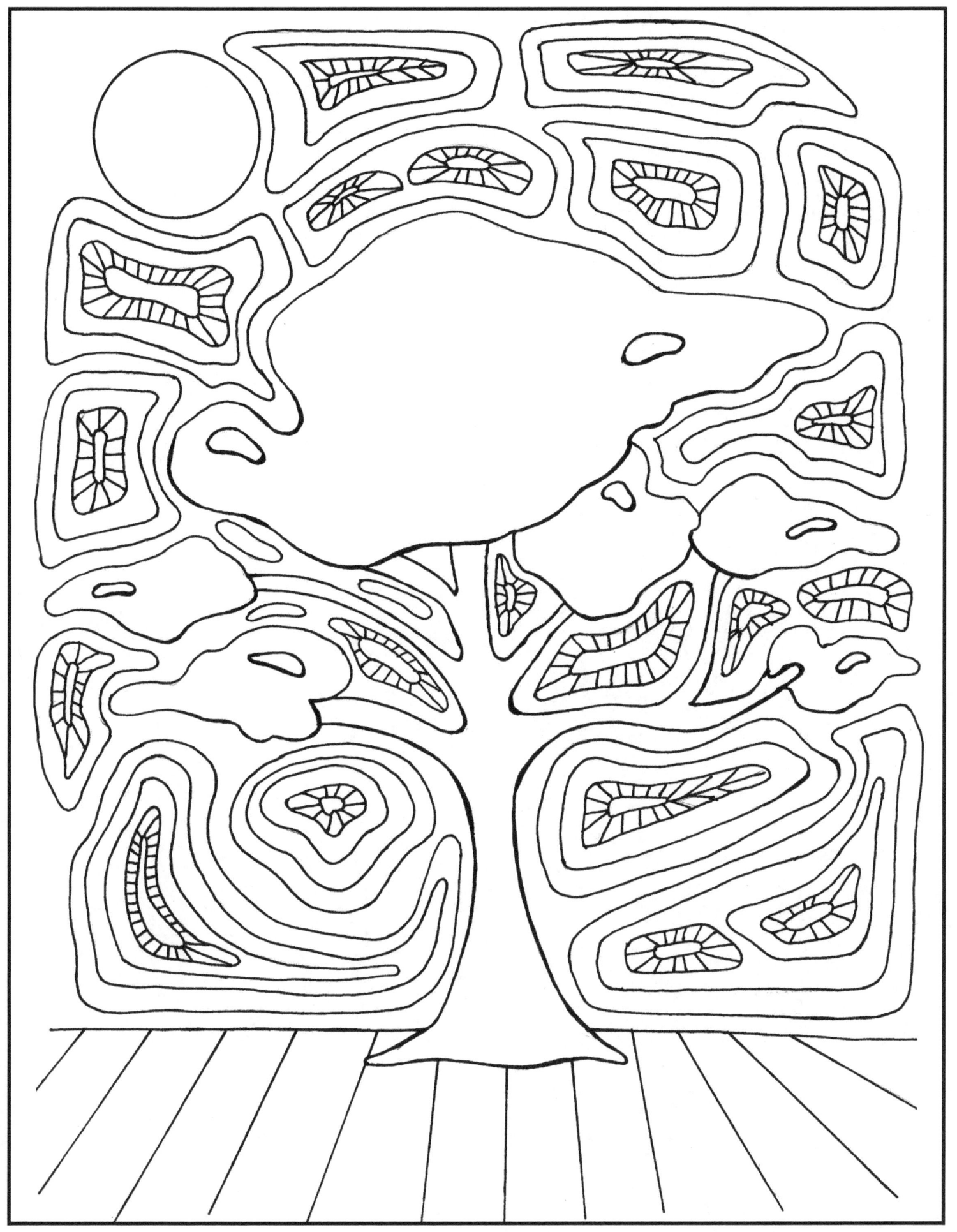

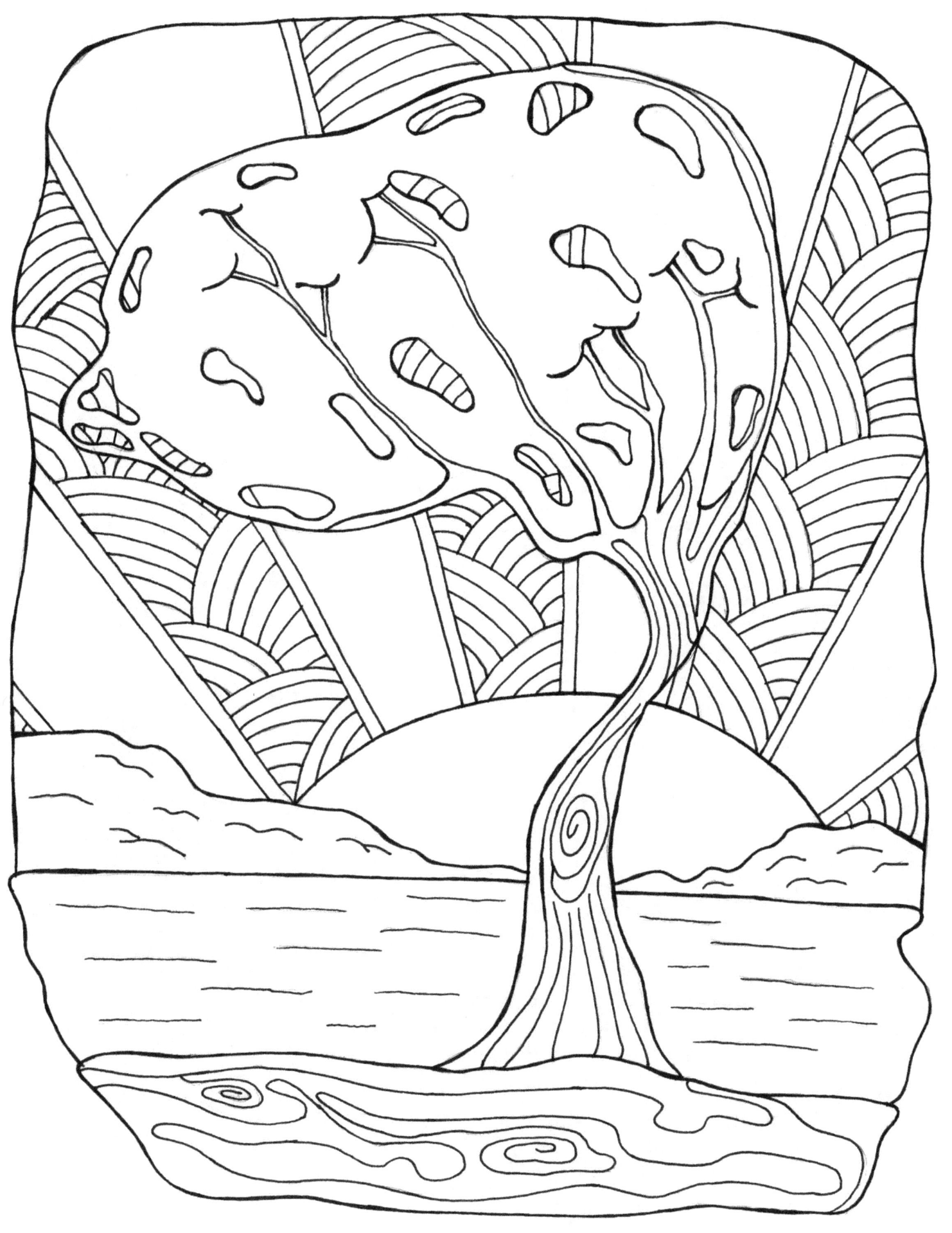

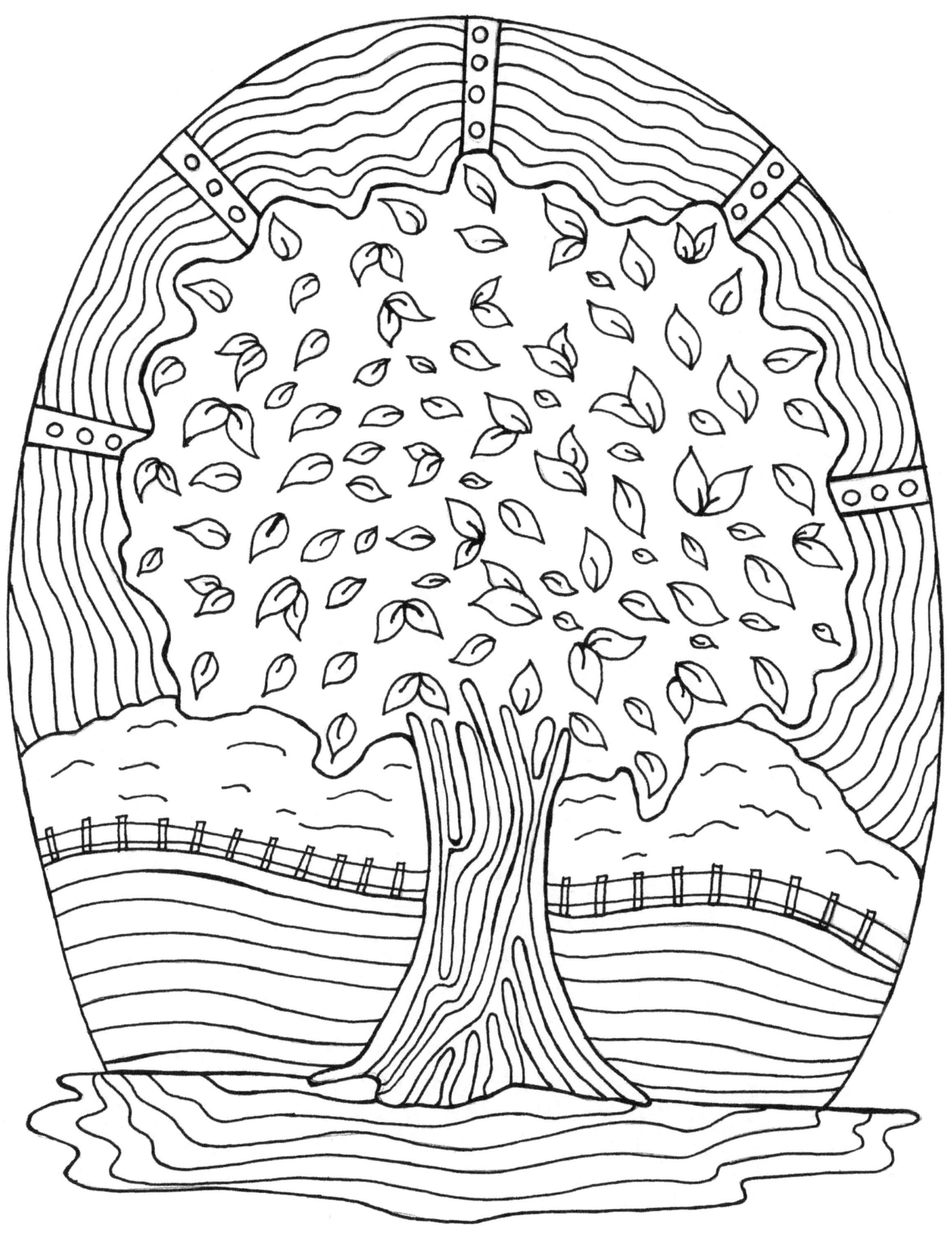

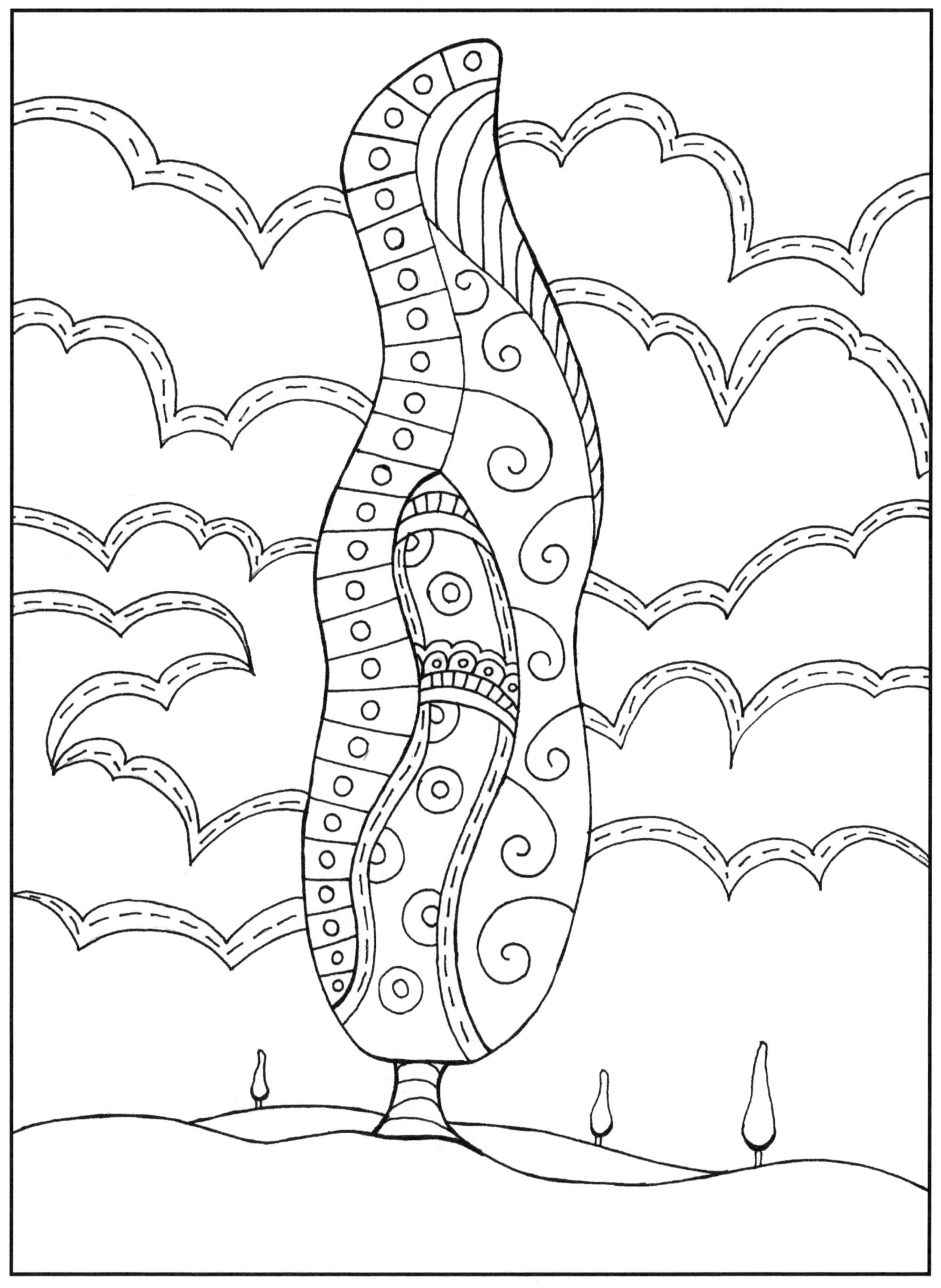

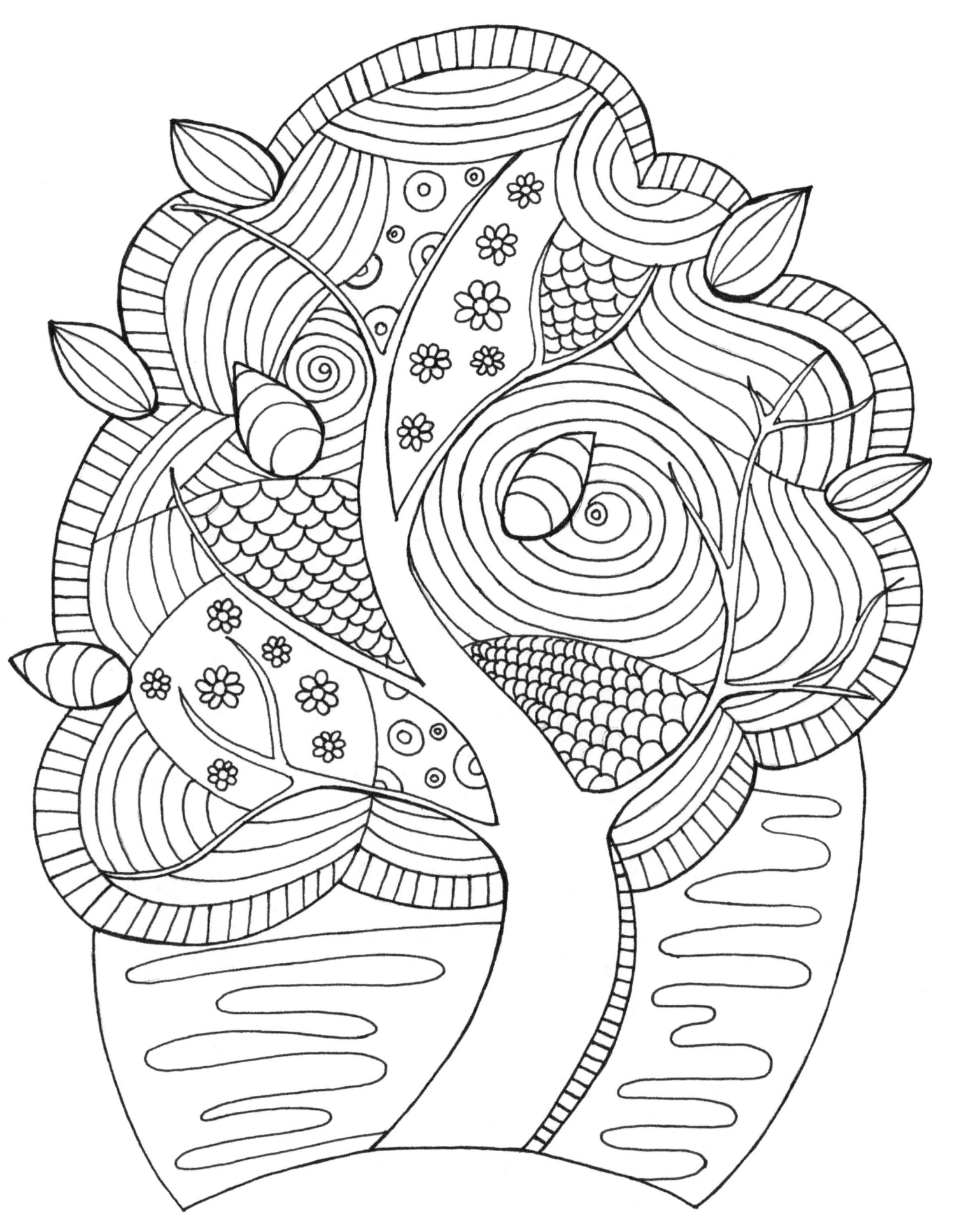

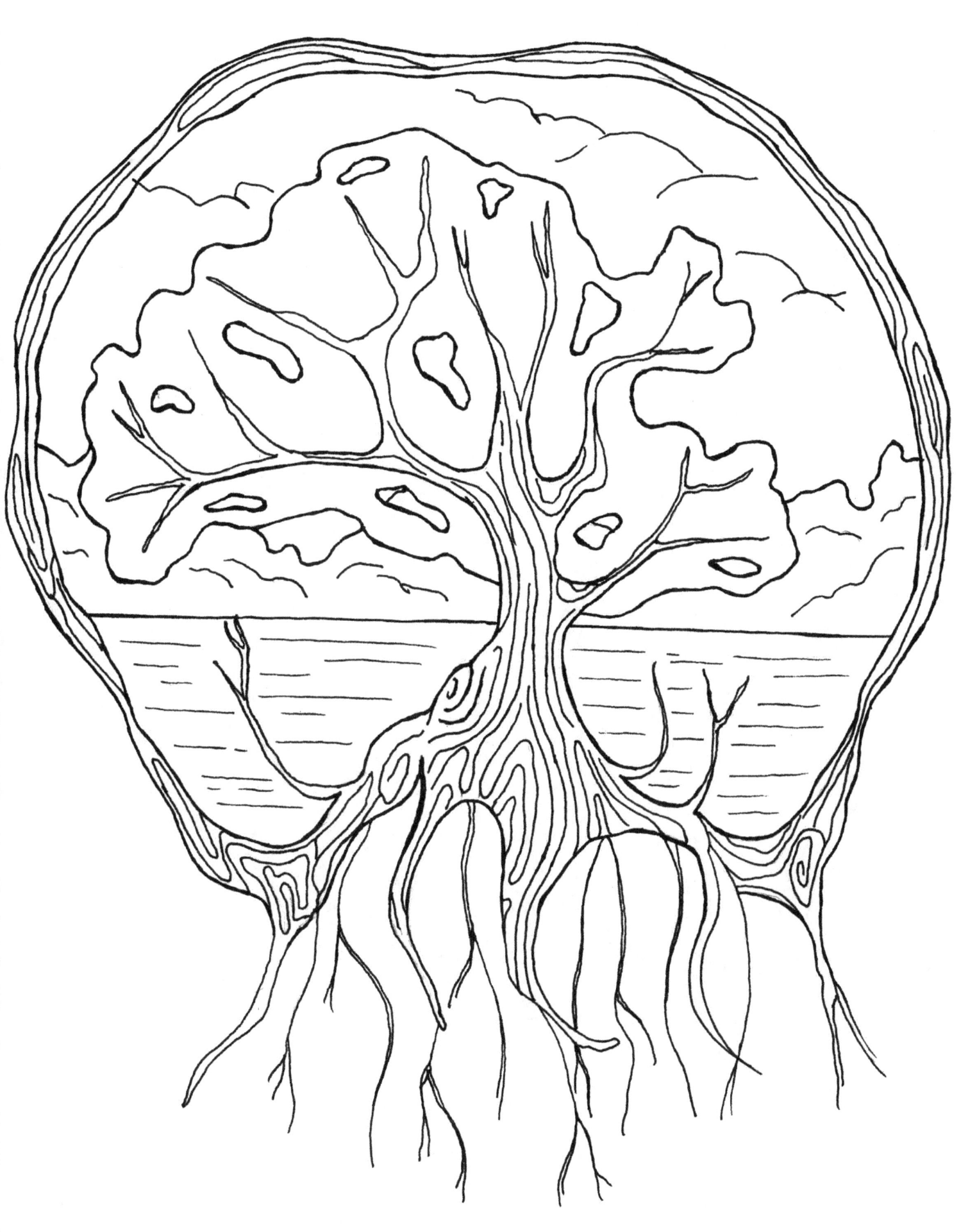

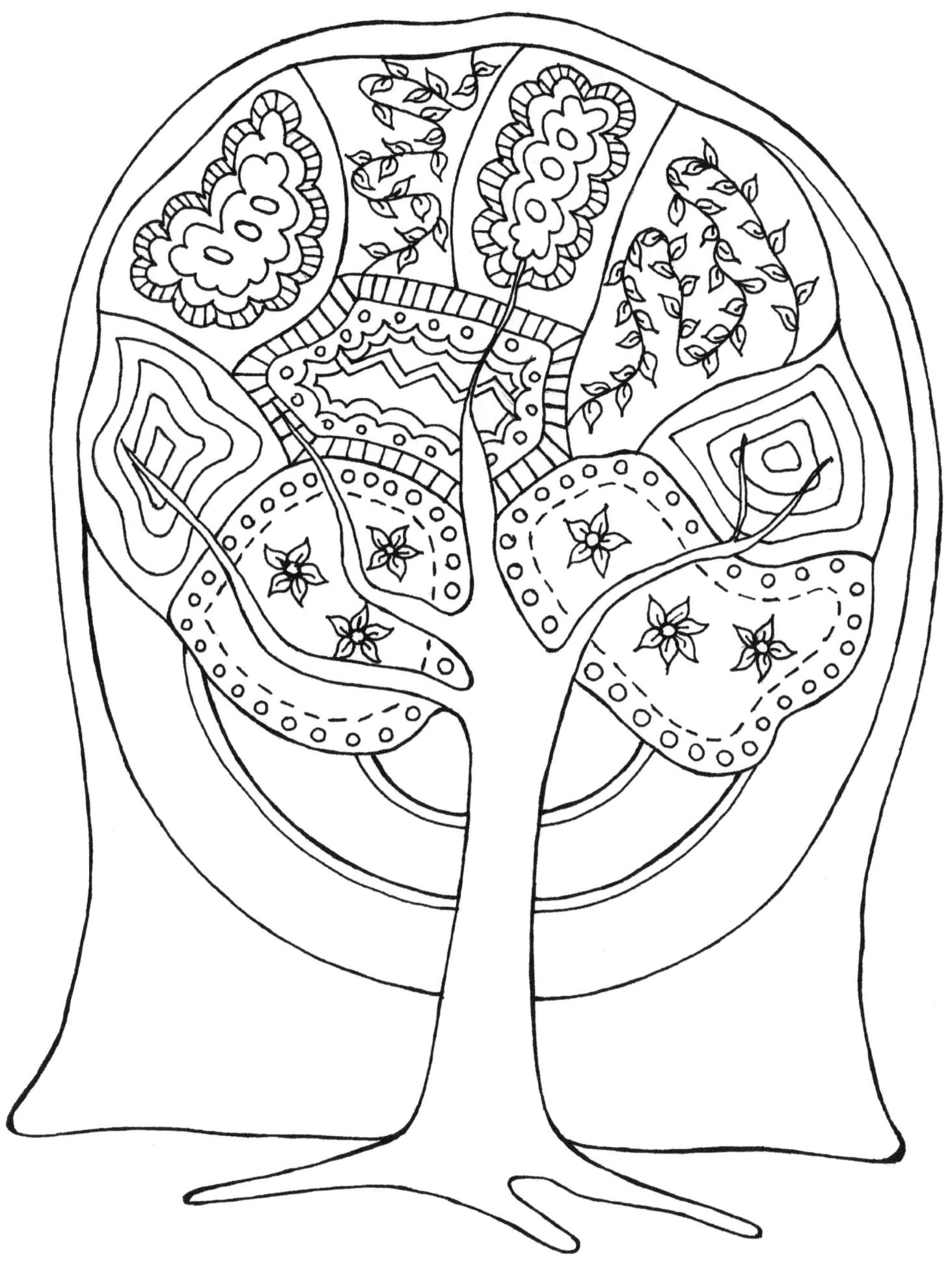

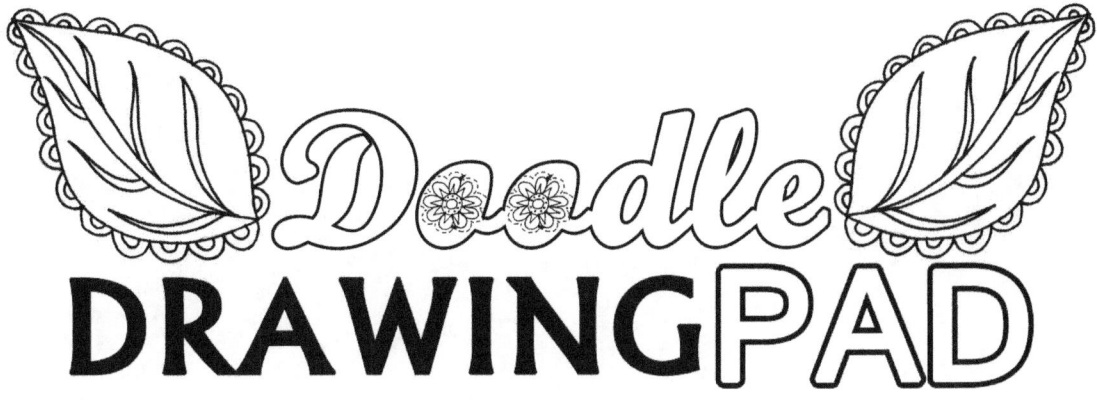

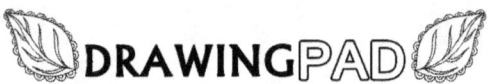

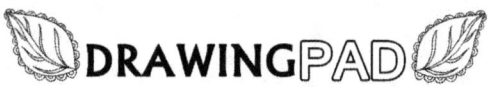

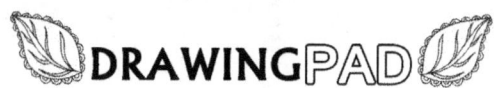

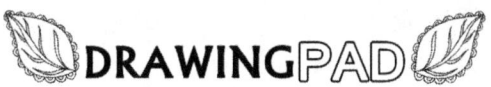

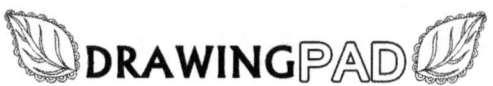

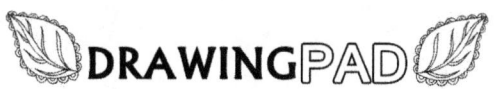

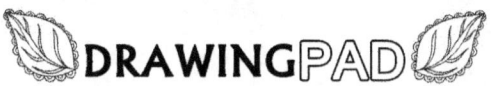

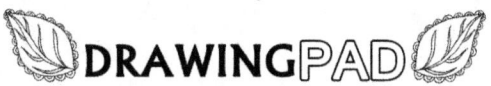

DRAWING

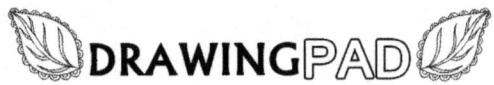